American Symbols
AND THEIR Meanings

THE
AMERICAN
FLAG

American Symbols
AND THEIR Meanings

THE AMERICAN FLAG

JOSEPH FERRY

MASON CREST PUBLISHERS
PHILADELPHIA

First printing

1 3 5 7 9 8 6 4 2

Library of Congress Cataloging-in-Publication Data
on file at the Library of Congress

ISBN 1-59084-026-7

Publisher's note: all quotations in this book come
from original sources, and contain the spelling and
grammatical inconsistencies of the original text.

American Symbols
AND THEIR **Meanings**

CONTENTS

THE IMPORTANCE OF AMERICAN SYMBOLS

Symbols are not merely ornaments to admire—they also tell us stories. If you look at one of them closely, you may want to find out why it was made and what it truly means. If you ask people who live in the society in which the symbol exists, you will learn some things. But by studying the people who created that symbol and the reasons why they made it, you will understand the deepest meanings of that symbol.

The United States owes its identity to great events in history, and the most remarkable American Symbols are rooted in these events. The struggle for independence from Great Britain gave America the Declaration of Independence, the Liberty Bell, the American flag, and other images of freedom. The War of 1812 gave the young country a song dedicated to the flag, "The Star-Spangled Banner," which became our national anthem. Nature gave the country its national animal, the bald eagle. These symbols established the identity of the new nation, and set it apart from the nations of the Old World.

To be emotionally moving, a symbol must strike people with a sense of power and unity. But it often takes a long time for a new symbol to be accepted by all the people, especially if there are older symbols that have gradually lost popularity. For example, the image of Uncle Sam has replaced Brother Jonathan, an earlier representation of the national will, while the Statue of Liberty has replaced Columbia, a woman who represented liberty to Americans in the early 19th century. Since then, Uncle Sam and the Statue of Liberty have endured and have become cherished icons of America.

Of all the symbols, the Statue of Liberty has perhaps the most curious story, for unlike other symbols, Americans did not create her. She was created by the French, who then gave her to America. Hence, she represented not what Americans thought of their country but rather what the French thought of America. It was many years before Americans decided to accept this French goddess of Liberty as a symbol for the United States and its special role among the nations: to spread freedom and enlighten the world.

This series of books is valuable because it presents the story of each of America's great symbols in a freshly written way and will contribute to the students' knowledge and awareness of them. It is to be hoped that this information will awaken an abiding interest in American history, as well as in the meanings of American symbols.

—Barry Moreno,
librarian and historian
Ellis Island/Statue of Liberty National Monument

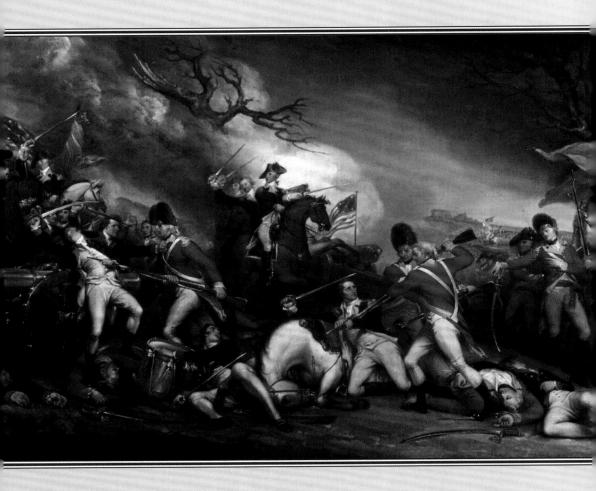

The newly created American flag flies at the left and center of this painting of a battle during the American War of Independence. The basic design of the American flag has not changed much in the more than 225 years since it was created in 1776.

A FLAG IS BORN

*I*n December 1775, as the possibility of a war for independence from England drew closer, a small group of important American colonial leaders met at a dinner party. Inevitably, the conversation turned to the question of a flag to represent the fight for freedom. A debate raged about what should be included on the flag until Benjamin Franklin offered a suggestion.

"While the *field* of our flag must be new in the details of its design, it need not be entirely new in its elements," suggested Franklin. "There is already in use a flag with which the English government is familiar and which it has not only recognized but also protected for more than half a century, the design of which can be readily modified, or rather extended, so as to most admirably suit our purpose."

Franklin was referring to the flag of the East India Company, which featured a field of alternating red and white stripes and the Cross of St. George—a red cross on a white field—in the upper left hand corner. His proposal was received enthusiastically by others in the group, including George Washington.

On January 1, 1776, only 20 days after the dinner, Washington *hoisted* this *national flag* for the first time at Prospect Hill, near Cambridge, Massachusetts. The flag had 13 alternating red and white stripes, with the *Union Jack* in the upper left corner. It was called the Grand Union flag. Later, it was called the Cambridge flag and the Continental flag. Of course, the Union Jack would eventually be replaced by the 13 white stars arranged in a circle on a blue background, signifying the 13 original colonies.

According to a book published by the U.S. Congress in 1989, the colors of the flag do not have special meaning. However, tradition has given the following meanings: White, purity and innocence; red, hardiness and valor; blue, vigilance, perseverance and justice.

But why was it so important to have a flag in the first place? After all, isn't a flag only a piece of cloth, attached to a pole with a bunch of different colors?

Actually, a flag is much more than that. A flag is a *symbol*. It represents people united by a common bond or cause. This bond can be military, state, religious, or national. The flag is often used as a rally-ing point, as it was for Washington's out-manned and under-supplied troops. It served as a source of

The Grand Union Flag was one of the earliest banners used by the Continental army.

pride, because it encompassed the hopes and ideals of the people it represented.

The first forms resembling modern flags were *banners*. They were made of cloth and displayed on a staff. Their main function was to indicate a person of importance, such as a king, a duke, or a military leader. Banners were mentioned in the Bible during the days of Solomon more than 3,000 years ago.

During the Middle Ages, a number of independent city-states in Italy used banners to establish an individ-ual symbol of identity. These cities were the first to use an extension of the banner as a symbol that would represent them. Thus, the concept of the flag was born.

It is generally accepted that the first real flag ever flown on what would become American soil was a white flag with a black raven on it. According to legend, this flag was carried by Erik the Red and his son, Leif

The commander-in-chief of the Continental Army during the Revolutionary War, George Washington was born February 22, 1732. As a young man, Washington worked as a surveyor, even though he had little or no formal schooling. Later, he became a tobacco farmer. During the French and Indian War, he fought with the British Army.

Washington's public opposition to unpopular British polices helped him win election as a Virginia delegate to the First Continental Congress in 1774 and the Second Continental Congress the following year.

In 1775, Congress placed Washington in charge of the Continental Army when fighting broke out between the British and citizens of Massachusetts.

After the end of the Revolutionary War, Washington was elected the country's first president in 1789. He left office in 1797 to retire to his estate in Mount Vernon, where he died on December 14, 1799.

Eriksson. They were Viking explorers believed to have landed in the Americas some 500 years before Christopher Columbus.

In the more than 225 years that have passed since the *colonists* declared themselves free of British rule, the American flag, with its red and white stripes and white stars neatly arranged on a blue background, has become perhaps the most recognizable symbol of freedom and democracy in the world. The flag represents not only the struggle by colonists for independence, but also the determination of settlers to push the frontier boundaries. It has also come to represent the thousands of American lives lost in battle in the country's history.

In a 1996 proclamation, President Bill Clinton had this to say about the American flag: "It continues to exemplify the profound commitment to freedom, equality, and opportunity made by our founders more than two centuries ago. Our flag's proud stars and stripes have long inspired our people, and its beautiful red, white, and blue design is known around the world as a beacon of liberty and justice."

Christopher Columbus plants his banner in the New World, 1492. The artist who created this 19th-century illustration made the crosses in Columbus's flags red; they actually were green. In the years after Columbus's voyage, the flags of many European nations have flown over different parts of North America.

THE FLAG EVOLVES

he flags that flew over America changed many times before the Stars and Stripes that we know today was created. Even before the first English settlers began arriving in the early 1600s, Native Americans used symbols to identify their tribes. Although some tribes were distinguished by their physical appearance, many developed their own symbols similar to those used in Europe and Asia thousands of years earlier.

In many cases, these symbols represented a tribe's "animal god," which was believed to be watching over them and lending "his" spirit to the members of "his tribe." These symbols usually were made of wood,

Native Americans symbols such as totem poles were used to distinguish different tribes.

stone, or leather and often were decorated with feathers or painted to create a distinctive symbol that was placed on a spear or lance. The "flag" was carried by a chief or his assistant during battle. In peacetime, it was placed in a conspicuous spot to mark a tribe's territory.

Some Indian tribes also used another type of *standard* known as a totem pole. This was a tall wooden carving decorated with feathers and various colors. But it was too large and heavy to be carried easily, so it mostly served as a stationary marker.

Starting in the late 15th century, a series of flags flew over what would become the United States.

In 1492, Christopher Columbus brought the Spanish flag to the New World. As he landed on the small island he called San Salvador, Columbus carried two flags. According to the journal he kept, "The Admiral brought out

A vexillologist is an expert in the history of flags.

the royal standard, and the captains went with two banners of the green cross, which the admiral flew on all the ships as a flag."

The first of these flags, the royal standard, was the flag of King Ferdinand and Queen Isabella, the sponsors of his expedition. It consisted of two castles and two lions. The other was a personal flag created especially for Columbus.

While it might be true to say that Erik the Red and his son Leif Eriksson were the first flag-bearers in North America, it was Columbus whose discovery made the greatest impact. Portugal, France, and England soon joined Spain in exploring the New World. Later, flags of the Netherlands, Sweden, and Russia were carried inland by exploring parties and were raised at forts and trading posts.

These flags are of interest because they flew over what are now the 50 states, but most of them did not make direct contributions to the development of the flag of the United States. They are more like distant relatives than parents or grandparents.

Throughout the 1500s, the Spanish flag dominated the Americas. Juan Ponce de León claimed Florida for Spain in 1513 and the Spanish flag flew there until 1763.

The British flag first arrived in the New World in 1497 when explorer John Cabot claimed much of the Atlantic Coast for England. In 1534, Frenchman Jacques Cartier sailed up the St. Lawrence River between the United

States and Canada and claimed nearly half the North American continent for France.

The Dutch flag was the next to fly in the New World when Henry Hudson sailed into New York harbor in 1609 and founded the Providence of New Netherlands 14 years later. The Swedish flag flew over what it now Wilmington, Delaware, beginning in 1638, when Peter Minuit organized the New Sweden Company. It flew until 1655, when Peter Stuyvesant, the governor of New Netherlands, marched into the small colony along the Delaware River and replaced it with the Dutch flag.

In 1664, an English task force assumed control of Stuyvesant's colonies. The Dutch flag was lowered and replaced by the **Union** Jack. At the same time, New Netherlands became known as New York.

The Union *Jack*, was flown at Jamestown, Virginia, starting in 1607, and at Plymouth, Massachusetts, starting in 1620. The first recorded change to the Union Jack that was made in America came in 1635, when the deeply religious Puritans, who objected to the use of a cross on the flag, removed it, leaving a blank white space in the corner. This flag was used for 50 years, after which the cross was restored with a green pine tree, signifying liberty, in the *canton*.

During the 1700s, several colonial flags were used in addition to the English flags. They usually were naval *ensigns* identifying a trade or company. For example, New York shippers used a white flag with a black beaver on it, symbolizing the fur trade. The New England pine tree was on several flags and appears on the state flag of Massachusetts today.

The French and Indian War was waged between 1754 and 1763. It united the British and American colonists in a common cause. At the end of the war, the British found themselves short of money, so they turned to their colonies in the New World for help. The colonists did not like the increased taxes and other changes forced on them from England. Their anger broke out in many forms, including the Boston Tea Party.

One of the first flags to fly over North America was the English flag. These three ships which brought English colonists to Jamestown, Virginia, in 1607 are flying both a white flag with the red cross of St. George and the Union Jack.

Some of the ways the colonists showed they were unhappy with British rule was by including unflattering additions to the Union Jack. Also, American patriots began flying flags of their own design. Often, these flags depicted a reptile native to the New World—the rattlesnake—coiled or stretched across the field with the words "Don't Tread on Me." The message to Britain was clear:

The rattlesnake was a popular motif on early flags of the American Revolution. This flag was carried by rebellious colonists in 1776.

the 13 colonies were not about to be bullied by the British monarchy. Other flags used the New England pine tree and various mottos. When the Revolutionary War began, the addition of both symbols to the Union Jack was widespread.

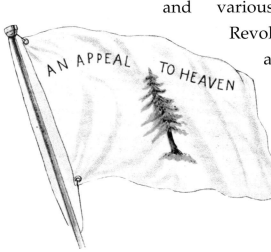

This pine tree flag was one of the early flags of the Continental navy. The motto shows that the American colonists felt God would support their rebellion.

The first flag to use 13 stripes to symbolize the 13 colonies is presumed to be the Markoe flag. This flag was commissioned by a man named Abraham Markoe, who was captain of the Philadelphia Troop of Light Horse in 1774. It consisted of a yellow silk field with silver fringe. Along the outer edges of the field there is a silver leaf design. In the center is an elaborate coat of arms, with an Indian on the left and an angel on the right. Below their feet is a white ribbon bearing the words: "For These We Strive." The British Union was originally painted in the upper left corner of the flag but with changing times and sentiments, an artist was instructed to paint 13 blue and silver stripes over the union to represent the united colonies.

The first flag to symbolize the colonies by using 13 stars is believed to be that used by a military battery in Providence, Rhode Island, called the United Train or Artillery. It was organized in 1775. The field was yellow with an anchor wrapped with rope, two cannons, scrolls with mottos, and a coiled rattlesnake circled by 13 blue, five-pointed stars.

Another pre-Revolutionary War flag using the 13 stars to symbolize the original colonies was carried by the First Rhode Island regiment. A white flag, it contained a blue canton with 13 stars.

While these flags served a valuable purpose for the people who designed and flew them, it would be the Stars and Stripes that would help unite a young nation against a common enemy.

Pedestrians walk past the Betsy Ross House in Philadelphia. It was here that the famed seamstress is supposed to have designed and created the first American flag. Whether or not the story of Betsy Ross is true remains a matter of debate today.

BETSY ROSS: FACT OR FICTION?

It didn't take long for dissatisfaction with the Grand Union flag to surface. The patriots were not happy with the flag because of its close connection to the British flag. During a visit to Philadelphia in June 1776, George Washington decided he needed a flag his Continental Army could rally around. John Hancock mentioned there was an *upholstery* shop near his house at Fourth and Arch Streets that might be able to help, so Washington went to see the owner, Betsy Ross.

Washington showed Betsy a rough sketch of what he had in mind: 13 stripes, just like the Grand Union Flag, but with 13 stars arranged in a circle instead of the Union

> Elizabeth Griscom—also called Betsy—was a fourth-generation American born on January 1, 1752. She was the eighth of 17 children born to Andrew Griscom, a Quaker carpenter, and Rebecca James, who came from a prominent merchant family.
>
> In November 1772, 21-year old Betsy Griscom eloped with John Ross, causing a deep split in her family. Two years after they were married, John and Betsy Ross started their own upholstery business in Philadelphia.
>
> It was at this upholstery shop that, according to legend, General George Washington commissioned Betsy to assemble the first American flag.
>
> With business slow because of the war with Britain, John Ross joined the Pennsylvania militia. In mid-January 1776, John Ross was badly wounded in an explosion while guarding a supply of ammunition. Betsy tried to nurse him back to health but John died a few days later.
>
> Betsy's second husband, Joseph Ashburn, a captain in the Continental Army, died in March 1782 in Old Mill Prison in England. He had been captured during a trip to the West Indies to get war supplies for the Revolutionary cause. Her third husband, John Claypoole, died in 1817. Betsy continued working as an upholsterer until 1827, when she was 75 years old. On January 30, 1836, she died at age 84.

Jack. Ross suggested that the stars have five points instead of six. Within a few days, she had assembled the first official United States flag as Washington had requested.

At least that's how the legend goes.

Although Betsy Ross's role in making the first American flag is based on stories by her daughters and nieces, historians are skeptical that it really happened that way. The first public mention that she might have had something to do with the flag did not come until 1870, when her grandson William J. Canby presented a paper to the Historical Society of Pennsylvania. He said that on many occasions before her death in 1836, Ross told her relatives the story of how she designed and sewed the first American flag.

In later years, historians and experts on the flag cast doubt on the story. The journals of the Continental Congress make no mention of the meeting. Although Washington loved to write letters and keep detailed diaries, there is no mention of him having a connection with designing or making the first American flag. None of the historians of the Revolutionary War make reference to the meeting, nor do any of the newspapers that were published in Philadelphia at the time.

It is more likely, historians say, that Francis Hopkinson, a patriot, lawyer, and congressman from New Jersey, designed the first Stars and Stripes.

Hopkinson was appointed to the Continental Navy Board on November 6, 1776. While serving on the board he turned his attention to designing the flag of the

> **The stars on the first American flag were arranged in a circle so that no one colony would be viewed above the others.**

United States. His decision to use stars is believed to have been the result of an experience in the war directly related to his property. In December 1776 a soldier fighting for the British had taken a book from the library of Hopkinson's house in Bordentown. On one page of the book was Hopkinson's bookplate, which had three six-pointed stars and his family motto, "Always Ready." The book was eventually returned to Hopkinson, but the soldier had written above and below the bookplate. The safe return of the book may have symbolized for Hopkinson the revival of American hope in the war against Britain.

In a letter to the Board of Admiralty in 1780, Hopkinson asserted that he had designed "the flag of the United States" as well as the Great Seal of the United States and other symbols of the new nation's government. He asked to be paid with "a quarter cask of public wine."

After long delays, including a congressional investigation, the U.S. Board of Treasury found that, "Hopkinson was not the only person consulted" on the matter of the flag design and therefore could not rightly claim the whole amount. Also, the board felt the public was entitled to

Today in Philadelphia, only the Liberty Bell and Independence Hall draw more visitors than the home of Betsy Ross. More than 250,000 tourists visit the Betsy Ross House annually. Betsy rented the Georgian-style house from 1773 to 1786. She lived there and ran the upholstery business out of the building. The house was built about 1740 and consists of two and a half floors and nine rooms.

Although the legend of Betsy Ross may not be true, the story remains popular today. In this illustration, George Washington reviews the flag Betsy has sewn for him in 1776.

these extra services from employees like Hopkinson, who drew high salaries.

As you can see, the exact origin of the Stars and Stripes is difficult to determine. It is most likely that the flag had no single designer but instead was a combination of ideas from many people. Any claim that the Stars and Stripes was used before June 14, 1777, when Congress passed the first law giving the country its first official flag, cannot be verified. No one has been able to produce a flag that conformed to Congress' specifications—"13 stripes, alternated red and white, and the Union [be] 13 stars white in a blue field representing a new constellation"—before that time.

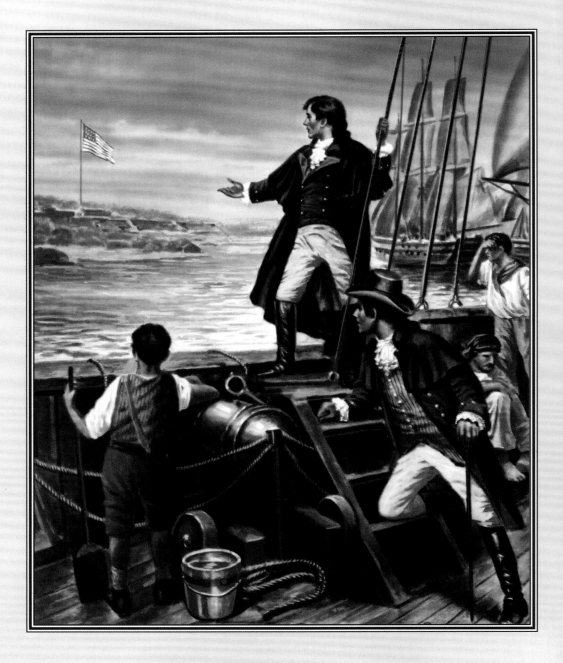

In this romantic drawing, Francis Scott Key gestures toward the flag waving over Fort McHenry in August 1814. Key witnessed a British attack on the fort at night, and was inspired when morning came and he saw the American flag still flying. His poem about the event was turned into a song that has become our national anthem.

A SONG FOR THE FLAG

fter war broke out in 1812 with Britain, all was not peaceful in Washington, D.C. On August 19, 1814, a British fleet entered Chesapeake Bay. Five days later, British troops invaded and captured Washington. When they set fire to the Capitol building and the White House, the flames were visible 40 miles away in Baltimore.

A thunderstorm at dawn kept the fires from spreading. The next day more buildings were burned and again a thunderstorm dampened the fires. Having done their work, the British troops returned to their ships in and around the Chesapeake Bay.

In the days following the attack on Washington, American forces prepared for an assault on Baltimore. They knew the attack would come by both land and sea. Word soon circulated that the British had carried off an elderly and much-loved town physician of Upper Marlboro, Dr. William Beanes, and were holding him captive on a British ship, the *Tonnant*. The townsfolk feared that Dr. Beanes would be hanged. They asked Francis Scott Key, a lawyer, for help. He agreed and arranged to have Colonel John Skinner, an American agent for prisoner exchange, accompany him for the negotiations.

On the morning of September 3, Key and Skinner set sail from Baltimore aboard a small boat flying a flag of truce approved by President James Madison. On the September 7, they found and boarded the *Tonnant.* The British first refused to release Dr. Beanes. But Key and Skinner produced a pouch of letters written by wounded British prisoners praising the care they were receiving from the Americans, among them Dr. Beanes. The British officers agreed to release the doctor. However, they would not let the three Americans go immediately because they had seen and heard too much about the plans for the attack on Baltimore. They were placed under guard and forced to wait for the end of the battle.

A year earlier Major George Armistead, the commander of Fort McHenry, had asked for a flag so big that "the British would have no trouble seeing it from a distance."

A group of children point at the Star-Spangled Banner, which for many years hung near the entrance to the National Museum of American History in Washington, D.C. In 1999 scientists began a conservation project that would keep the flag from falling apart.

Two officers were sent to the Baltimore home of Mary Young Pickersgill, a "maker of colours," and commissioned the flag. Mary and her 13-year-old daughter

A Baptist minister named Francis Bellamy wrote the Pledge of Allegiance in August 1892. It was published in the September 8 issue of *The Youth's Companion*, the leading family magazine of its time.

His original pledge read this way: "I pledge allegiance to my flag and to the Republic for which it stands, one nation, indivisible, with liberty and justice for all." He considered adding the word "equality" to the pledge, but he knew that many people of that era were against equality for women and African Americans.

In 1923 and 1924, the National Flag Conference changed the pledge's words from "my flag" to "the Flag of the United States of America." Bellamy didn't like the changes, but they were made anyway.

In 1954, Congress added the words "under God" to the pledge, making it both a patriotic oath and a public prayer.

Caroline, working in an upstairs front bedroom, used 400 yards of best quality wool bunting. They cut 15 stars that measured two feet from point to point. Eight red and seven white stripes, each two feet wide, were cut. Laying out the material on the floor of a brewery, the flag was sewn together. By August 1813 it was finished. The flag measured 30 by 42 feet and cost $405.90.

At 7 A.M. on the morning of September 13, 1814, the British bombardment began, and the flag was ready to meet the enemy. The bombardment continued for 25 hours. The British fired 1,500 bombshells that weighed as much as 220 pounds apiece. These bombs carried fuses that would supposedly cause them to explode when they hit the target. But the fuses weren't very dependable and the bombs often blew up in midair. From special small boats the British fired new rockets that traced wobbly arcs of red flame across the sky. The Americans had sunk 22 vessels, so a close approach by the British was not possible. That evening the bombardment stopped, but at about 1 A.M. on September 14, the British guns roared back to life, lighting the rainy night sky with grotesque fireworks.

Key, Colonel Skinner, and Dr. Beanes nervously watched the battle. They knew that as long as the shelling continued, Fort McHenry had not surrendered. But long before daylight there came a sudden and mysterious silence. What the three Americans did not know was that the British had decided to give up the attack on the fort. Judging Baltimore to be too costly a prize, the British officers ordered a retreat.

In the predawn darkness, Key waited for the sight that would end his anxiety—the joyous sight of General Armistead's great flag blowing in the breeze. When at last daylight came, the flag was still there!

Being an amateur poet and having been inspired by the scene, Key began to write on the back of a letter he had in his pocket. Sailing back to Baltimore he composed more lines. Key's brother-in-law took the poem to a printer and copies were circulated around Baltimore under the title "Defence of Fort M'Henry." Two of these copies survive. It was printed in a newspaper for the first time in the *Baltimore Patriot* on September 20, 1814. It was soon reprinted in newspapers as far away as Georgia and New Hampshire. To the verses was added a note,

Stephen Driver, a ship's captain from Massachusetts, is credited with coining the name "Old Glory" for the American flag. In 1831, as he was leaving on one of his many voyages, some friends presented him with a beautiful 24-star flag. As the banner opened to the ocean breeze for the first time, Driver called it "Old Glory."

Driver retired to Nashville in 1837, taking the flag from his sea days with him. By the time the Civil War erupted, most everyone in and around Nashville recognized Captain Driver's "Old Glory." When Tennessee seceded from the Union, rebels were determined to destroy his flag, but they could not find it.

Then on February 25, 1862, Union forces captured Nashville and raised the American flag over the capitol building. It was rather small, and immediately folks began asking Captain Driver if "Old Glory" still existed. Happy to have soldiers with him this time, Captain Driver went home and began ripping at the seams of his bedcover. As the stitches holding the quilt top to the batting unraveled, the onlookers peered inside and saw the 24-starred original "Old Glory."

Captain Driver gently gathered up the flag and returned with the soldiers to the capitol. Though he was 60 years old, Captain Driver climbed up to the tower to replace the smaller banner with his beloved flag. The Sixth Ohio Regiment cheered and saluted—and later adopted the nickname "Old Glory" as their own, telling and retelling the story of Captain Driver's flag.

Captain Driver's grave is located in the old Nashville City Cemetery. It is one of three places where the flag of the United States may be flown 24 hours a day.

"Tune: 'Anacreon in Heaven.'" In October a Baltimore actor sang Key's new song in a public performance and called it "The Star-Spangled Banner."

Immediately popular, it remained just one of several patriotic songs until it was finally adopted as our national anthem on March 3, 1931. But the actual words were not included in the legal documents that officially made "The Star-Spangled Banner" the national anthem. Key himself had written several versions with slight variations, so discrepancies in the exact wording still occur.

On January 1, 1876, the beloved flag went on view for the first time since it flew over Fort McHenry. The display occurred at the Old State House in Philadelphia, as part of the nation's centennial celebration. It was donated to the Smithsonian Institution early in the 20th century, and since 1964 it has been on display at the Smithsonian's Museum of American History.

However, the years have taken a toll on the Star-Spangled Banner. In 1994 museum curators realized that the flag was in bad shape. It was taken down in December 1998 and carefully cleaned. A three-year project to conserve the flag began in June 1999. Visitors to the Smithsonian can see the technicians carefully working to preserve the grand old flag.

A woman waves the flag during a Veterans Day parade. To many people, the stars and stripes holds great importance as a symbol of America.

RIGHT OR DISRESPECT?

The flag has been a very visible part of many defining moments in American history. When the Marines captured Mount Suribachi, on the island of Iwo Jima, during World War II, a photographer captured several of them planting a flag in the soil. This picture of the flag-raising has become a stirring symbol of American victory. When man first walked on the moon in 1969, an American flag was placed on the surface as millions of people around the world watched. When explorer Robert Peary became the first man to reach the North Pole in 1909, he scattered pieces of the American flag on the frozen ground.

On July 20, 1969, Neil Armstrong accomplished the unthinkable—he stepped from the lunar module named *Eagle* to the surface of the moon! It was the culmination of many years of work by thousands of scientists. As he touched the moon for the first time, Armstrong, who was 39 years old, uttered a phrase that would become famous: "That's one small step for a man, one giant leap for mankind."

After conducting a few tests, Armstrong was joined by fellow astronaut Edwin "Buzz" Aldrin on the moon's surface. With the whole world watching, the two men performed a very important task. They produced an American flag and planted it on the moon. However, unlike previous explorers who claimed land for their countries, Armstrong and Aldrin did not claim the moon for the United States. In fact, the U.S. and several other countries had signed a treaty making the moon *terra nullilus*—no man's land.

The Stars and Stripes hold a great meaning for most Americans, especially those who have served in war and saw friends and comrades killed or wounded in battle.

Grown men and women have been known to weep at the sight of the flag being carried down the street in a parade.

Whenever a symbol such as the American flag represents such deep emotions, opponents will attack it, both physically and verbally, as a way of showing their displeasure. After all, isn't that what the colonists did to the flag of Great Britain before and during the Revolutionary War?

Because the flag is a powerful symbol of the nation, many Americans treat it with the courtesy and respect usually reserved for an honored person.

Of course, this custom is not always respected by everyone. The flag has been attacked by people hostile to American deeds and policies. It is not uncommon to see protesters from other countries burning the American flag because they disagree with U.S. actions. In other instances, the flag has been treated casually and used by advertisers and manufacturers to sell products.

Despite the importance of the flag, the United States government has taken a relaxed approach to questions about its abuse. Over the years, rules for properly handling and displaying the

> The American Flag should never be *dipped* to any person or thing. It should be flown upside down only as a distress signal. When the flag is lowered it should not touch the ground or any other object; it should be received with waiting hands. To store the flag it should be folded neatly and ceremoniously.

flag have been developed, although not by the government. Throughout most of the flag's existence these rules have been neither official nor enforced. It was not until 1942 that Congress adopted an official Flag Code, most of which was written by patriotic organizations such as the American Legion.

In 1968, when protests against U.S. involvement in the Vietnam War were at their peak, the American flag was a convenient target. Frequently, the flag was burned by large, angry crowds in front of television cameras in order to get attention.

An angry mob burns the the flags of the United States and India during a rally in June 1999. The flag is burned to indicate displeasure with U.S. policies. Over the years, amendments to the Constitution that would make it against the law for American citizens to burn the flag have been proposed, but not passed.

It was at this time that Congress passed the first federal law declaring desecration of the flag a crime. But there has been a great deal of doubt and debate about the law.

As recently as March 2000, the U.S. Senate turned down an amendment to the

> The U.S. Flag Code says the flag, when it is no longer a fitting emblem for display, should be destroyed in a dignified way. In many communities, organizations such as the American Legion and Boy Scouts conduct ceremonies to retire flags on Flag Day (June 14).

U.S. Constitution that would have given Congress the power to ban desecration of the flag. A similar attempt fell short in 1995. Supporters of the amendment say the flag is a sacred symbol of American values that deserves constitutional protection. Opponents do not want to tamper with the free-speech guarantees in the Bill of Rights to deal with relatively rare instances of flag burning.

However, Americans on both sides of the debate rallied around the flag on September 11, 2001. On that date, terrorists flew hijacked passenger airplanes into the World Trade Center Buildings in New York City, as well as the Pentagon in Washington, D.C.

In the next few days, as rescue crews struggled through the wreckage of the Pentagon building, several men climbed to the roof of the building, where they unfurled a large American flag. To all Americans, despite the terrorist attack, the Stars and Stripes remain an important symbol of freedom and democracy.

1776 The Grand Union flag is displayed on Prospect Hill on January 1; according to legend, Betsy Ross creates the first American flag.

1777 On June 14, the Continental Congress sets rules for the flag of the United States, with 13 stripes and 13 stars representing Delaware, Pennsylvania, New Jersey, Georgia, Connecticut, Massachusetts, Maryland, South Carolina, New Hampshire, Virginia, New York, North Carolina and Rhode Island.

1795 Flag with 15 stars and 15 stripes debuts (the states of Vermont and Kentucky are added).

1814 Francis Scott Key writes "The Star Spangled Banner" on September 14. It is later set to music, and officially becomes the national anthem in 1931.

1818 Flag with 20 stars debuts (Tennessee, Ohio, Louisiana, Indiana, and Mississippi are added). Two stripes are removed, setting the number of stripes at 13.

1819 Flag with 21 stars debuts (Illinois is added).

1820 Flag with 23 stars debuts (Alabama and Maine are added).

1822 Flag with 24 stars debuts (Missouri is added).

1836 Flag with 25 stars debuts (Arkansas is added).

1837 Flag with 26 stars debuts (Michigan is added).

1845 Flag with 27 stars debuts (Florida is added).

1846 Flag with 28 stars debuts (Texas is added).

1847 Flag with 29 stars debuts (Iowa is added).

1848 Flag with 30 stars debuts (Wisconsin is added).

1851 Flag with 31 stars debuts (California is added).

1858 Flag with 32 stars debuts (Minnesota is added).

1859 Flag with 33 stars debuts (Oregon is added).

1861 Flag with 34 stars debuts (Kansas is added); first Confederate Flag (the Stars and Bars) is adopted in Montgomery, Alabama.

1863 Flag with 35 stars debuts (West Virginia is added).

1865 Flag with 36 stars debuts (Nevada is added)

1867 Flag with 37 stars debuts (Nebraska is added).

1869 First flag appears on a postage stamp.

1877 Flag with 38 stars debuts (Colorado is added).

1890 Flag with 43 stars debuts (North Dakota, South Dakota, Montana, Washington, and Idaho are added).

1891 Flag with 44 stars debuts (Wyoming is added).

1892 "A Pledge to the Flag," by Francis Bellamy, is published in a magazine called *The Youth's Companion;* his words are later renamed "The Pledge of Allegiance."

1896 Flag with 45 stars debuts (Utah is added).

1908 Flag with 46 stars debuts (Oklahoma is added).

1909 Robert Peary places a flag his wife sewed atop the North Pole, and leaves pieces of another flag along his route.

1912 Flag with 48 stars debuts (New Mexico and Arizona are added).

1945 The flag that flew over Pearl Harbor on December 7, 1941, is flown over the White House on August 14, when the Japanese accept surrender terms.

1949 President Harry S. Truman signs a bill setting June 14 of each year as Flag Day.

1959 Flag with 49 stars debuts (Alaska is added).

1960 Flag with 50 stars debuts (Hawaii is added).

1963 Flag placed on top of Mount Everest by Barry Bishop.

1969 The American flag is placed on the moon by Neil Armstrong and Edwin "Buzz" Aldrin on July 20.

1995 The Flag Desecration Constitutional Amendment is narrowly defeated in the Senate on December 12. The Amendment would have made burning the flag a punishable crime.

2000 In March, the Flag Desecration Constitutional Amendment is again defeated.

banner—originally a large, rectangular medieval flag; today, this refers to any rectangular piece of fabric used as a symbol.

canton—originally a word describing the four quarters of a shield and always less than one-quarter of the total surface of a flag. In modern times, as used when referring to flags, it means the area in the top corner next to the pole or staff.

colonist—early settlers in the New World were called colonists because they lived in one of the 13 colonies.

dipped—when a flag is lowered slightly and immediately raised again as a form of salute.

ensign—originally, a standard, badge emblem, symbol, or sign. It may also be a military or naval flag or banner.

field—the background of the flag surface. The Stars and Stripes has a blue field in the canton, with the balance of the field comprised of horizontal red and white stripes.

hoist—the act of raising the flag. Also, the height of the flag from top to bottom, or the area of the flag closest to the pole.

jack—a naval flag smaller than an ensign and flown at a ship's bow as a mark of distinction or to show nationality. The American Jack is the canton of the Stars and Stripes, a blue field containing 50 five-pointed stars.

national flag—the official flag of a country or nation.

standard—a flag or banner that is adopted as an emblem or symbol by a nation.

symbol—an item that represents or stands for something else.

union—the combining of two or more entities into one. In the flag of Great Britain, for example, the union is a combination of the St. George Cross, the St. Andrew Cross, and the St. Patrick Cross. In the American flag, the union refers to the canton, or the union of the states represented by the stars.

Union Jack—the national flag of Great Britain.

upholstery—material used to make a soft covering, such as a seat.

FURTHER READING

DeBarr, Candice, and Jack Bonkowske. *Saga of the American Flag*. New York: Harbinger House, 1990.

Grant, Nancy. *Old Glory: A History and Celebration*. New York: Crescent Books, 1992

Gray, Susan. *The American Flag*. Minneapolis: Compass Point Books, 2001.

Hinrichs, Kit, and Delphine Hirasuna. *Long May She Wave: A Graphic History of the American Flag*. Berkeley, Calif.: Ten Speed Press, 2001.

Parish, Thomas. *The American Flag, The Symbol of Our Nation Throughout Its History*. New York: Simon and Schuster, 1973.

Smith, Whitney. *The American Flag*. New York: Friedman/Fairfax Publishers, 2001.

INTERNET RESOURCES

History of the American Flag
http://www.usflag.org
http://www.icss.com/usflag/toc.html

The Star-Spangled Banner
http://www.150.si.edu/chap3/flag.htm
http://www.flaghouse.com
http://americanhistory.si.edu/ssb/2_home/fs2.html

Flag-burning Constitutional Amendment
http://www.cfa-inc.org

North American Vexillogical Association
http://www.nava.com

PICTURE CREDITS

BARRY MORENO has been librarian and historian at the Ellis Island Immigration Museum and the Statue of Liberty National Monument since 1988. He is the author of *The Statue of Liberty Encyclopedia*, which was published by Simon and Schuster in October 2000. He is a native of Los Angeles, California. After graduation from California State University at Los Angeles, where he earned a degree in history, he joined the National Park Service as a seasonal park ranger at the Statue of Liberty; he eventually became the monument's librarian. In his spare time, Barry enjoys reading, writing, and studying foreign languages and grammar. His biography has been included in *Who's Who Among Hispanic Americans*, *The Directory of National Park Service Historians*, *Who's Who in America*, and *The Directory of American Scholars*.

JOSEPH FERRY is a veteran journalist who has written for several newspapers in Philadelphia and the surrounding suburbs. He lives in Sellersville, Pennsylvania, with his wife and three children. His other books in Mason Crest's AMERICAN SYMBOLS AND THEIR MEANINGS series are *The Vietnam Veterans Memorial, The National Anthem,* and *The Jefferson Memorial.*